Studies in Political and Social Processes

A Discussion with

Gerald R. Ford

The American Presidency

A Discussion with

Gerald R. Ford

The American Presidency

Held on March 25, 1977
at the American Enterprise Institute for Public Policy Research
Washington, D.C.

ISBN 0-8447-3257-5

AEI Studies 159

Library of Congress Catalog Card No. 77-80274

Printed in the United States of America

CONTENTS

FOREWORD

Not all scholars have the advantage of confronting the subject of their research face to face. Dumas Malone, for example, mused eloquently in a recent interview on what it might be like to meet with the subject of his monumental biography, Thomas Jefferson.

The American Enterprise Institute takes some pride, therefore, in bringing together the thirty-eighth President of the United States, the Honorable Gerald R. Ford, and a group of students of the American presidency. The occasion was the former President's first return to Washington after leaving office, when he took up his responsibilities as the Distinguished Fellow of the American Enterprise Institude. In the first of AEI's expanded academic outreach programs, he met with students of a course on the American presidency given by Professor Fred I. Greenstein at Princeton University. In the next year, he will attend similar seminars and conferences on campuses throughout the country.

In discussions such as this one, President Ford offers us a double perspective on the presidency, telling us how it appeared during his long career in Congress and also how it appears now, in retrospect. As noted in the following discussion, an earlier President remarked about his office, "If you can't stand the heat, get out of the kitchen." It is our earnest hope that discussions such as this will help to shed some light on the "heat" of the U.S. presidency.

June 1977

WILLIAM J. BAROODY
President
American Enterprise Institute
for Public Policy Research

1

A Discussion with
GERALD R. FORD

FRED I. GREENSTEIN, Henry Luce professor of politics, law, and society, Princeton University: I would like to thank you for taking time from your busy schedule to invite students from my Princeton presidency course and resident scholars at the American Enterprise Institute to discuss the presidency with you.

To start off, Harry Truman remarked about the presidency, "If you can't stand the heat, get out of the kitchen." I would like to ask how one bears the emotional strain of being President of the United States, and whether you found it an emotional strain.

PRESIDENT FORD: I'm sure every President handles it differently. Some react one way, and some need a different way, a different outlet. I was able to handle the long work schedule—which in my case extended from about 5:30 in the morning until dinner at maybe 7:30 at night, and with some work afterwards.

I had to have a physical outlet—swimming or some other activity—that burned up those juices that were not normally consumed during the day. That activity gave me a relief, a change of pace, so to speak.

But I found that the pressures I had read about were not nearly as severe as I expected, as long as my staff organized them properly.

AUSTIN RANNEY, resident scholar, American Enterprise Institute: As we all know, you served for some twenty-five years or more as a member of the House of Representatives and rose to the leadership of your party. In the House of Representatives, you dealt with Presidents of both parties on a variety of issues, and I'm sure you had a view of the office of the presidency at the time you were a leader in the Congress. Then, as few others in history have done, you became the leader of the executive branch. What were your views of the presidency when you were a member of the House, and how did they change—if they did at all—after you became President?

PRESIDENT FORD: I first became a member of the House of Representatives under President Truman, but I was so junior I had little exposure to the White House organization or to the President. Then, I became a bit more senior, and I had more opportunity to participate in meetings with President Eisenhower on foreign policy and military appropriations, subjects where I had developed some expertise because I was on those two subcommittees of the Appropriations Committee.

I really got first-hand exposure to the organization of the White House when my former colleague in the House, Jack Kennedy, became President. I had moved up the ladder sufficiently so I was invited down to either individual meetings with President Kennedy or bipartisan meetings with him. Then, of course, I also had meetings with President Johnson and President Nixon.

When I was in the House and anticipated nothing other than being a member of the Congress, I observed how each of those Presidents seemed to organize the White House differently. President Nixon had a very tightly held organization, with a chief of staff who ran the total operation. President Johnson seemed to have more intimate contact than President Nixon had with the various people that reported from Defense and the domestic side. He seemed to be more involved himself. I used to comment, one way or another, on both systems.

When I became President—not having anticipated that I would— I initially felt that what I perceived as the Johnson organization was preferable, with seven or eight different people within the White House reporting directly to the President. But I must say, after six months I did find that a President needs one person who at least coordinates people such as the President's assistant for national security affairs, the head of the Domestic Council, the head of the Economic Policy Board, et cetera. Somebody had to organize the day's schedule and the flow of paperwork.

In the last eighteen months, I ended up with an open oval office. Anybody who had a particular problem could come in and see me but had to be channeled through at least one person who had some control over the schedule. Every day, I approved the schedule of people coming in, but somebody in a central office at least gave me options as to whom I wanted to see or the subjects I would discuss during the ten or twelve hours that I was in the oval office each day.

JEFF SIEGEL, student: What would you say are the most important qualities inside the man for being a successful President?

PRESIDENT FORD: I believe that integrity is mandatory. I mean in the broadest sense, not just in matters of money. That transcends everything else, really. If a President has integrity in the widest possible connotation of the word, I think he gets off to a good start.

There are other important traits. I think a President has to have confidence in himself—not an overbearing confidence but confidence in a decision after he has thought it out and has had the options presented to him. I happen to think that confidence is, to a substantial degree, predicated on common sense—not just on intellectual capabilities but on how to evaluate, how to judge, how to read into something, whether it is on paper or the spoken word. A President must develop a sense of security when he has made a decision involving two options or five options, after having the case presented and after looking at the alternatives. He has to be confident that he has had all of the tools available, that he has used them, and that he has selected the right one.

RICHARD DEVANE, student: Mr. President, in structuring your White House staff, how important was it to you to have people who represented a variety of viewpoints—who were sort of inhouse critics—even at the expense of some discord?

PRESIDENT FORD: That is a technique I used even when I was the minority leader in the House of Representatives. I had as the minority leader's team, so to speak, the people who represented the varying parts of the spectrum in the Republican party. We used to have some healthy arguments among the House Republican leaders, because some were allegedly liberal and some were categorized as conservative.

I tried to have the same diversity in my top cabinet selections and in my top staff selections for the White House. I can recall vividly some very heated conversations between three or four of the cabinet officers. I don't think they would object to my revealing their names. The attorney general had certain views on several matters, and Bill Coleman, who was the secretary of transportation, had a somewhat different viewpoint.

These discussions would go back and forth, but I think they were always intellectually honest and firm. They would become a little heated at times, but always in the right tone. I was the beneficiary of these discussions. I think any President ought to expose himself to that kind of dialogue between very intelligent people who have slightly different viewpoints.

BOB CHARTENER, student: Mr. President, do you feel that during the Mayaguez incident there was this type of intercourse between your advisors, that you did explore all of the possibilities?

PRESIDENT FORD: I'm sure that we explored all of the possibilities. That was an incident that arose most unexpectedly. We discussed why it came up without some forewarning but that's a long story. I think there was ample reason why it came up as it did. We held a number of National Security Council meetings, with the secretary of state, the secretary of defense, the chairman or a representative of the joint chiefs of staff, and the head of the CIA. We had ample representation in those NSC meetings, so the best options were presented.

First, of course, we tried the diplomatic approach, but the Cambodians were inaccessible diplomatically even then; they are even less accessible now. We went through the various channels—the United Nations, the People's Republic of China, and several other, unofficial sources.

When that was not successful, we considered the military options, and they were significantly different. In this instance the National Security Council gave the President the kind of options he ought to have had.

JILL BARON, student: Mr. President, do you feel that a woman is capable of handling the duties and responsibilities, the emotional strain, and the long work schedule of the presidency?

PRESIDENT FORD: Absolutely.

MS. BARON: And do you foresee a woman President of the United States in the next thirty years?

PRESIDENT FORD: I already answered the first part of the question. I think women today are qualified intellectually, physically, emotionally, and otherwise to handle the job. In my opinion, there will be a sequence of steps in getting a woman into the oval office: it won't be by nomination as President at a convention. I think a major political party will select a woman as vice president, and she and her presidental running mate will be elected. Then during the term of office, the President will pass away, and the woman will become the President in that way. And it will happen more quickly than waiting for the other process to take place. I honestly believe it will happen in the next thirty years. After the dam is broken, if she performs well, then I think it will be quite a different circumstance.

WARREN STONE, student: Mr. President, do you think the massive expansion of the presidency since Franklin D. Roosevelt and the centralization of power in the White House need to be checked?

PRESIDENT FORD: There were some excesses during World War II that obviously had to be checked through centralization, and that trend continued after World War II. I was in the Congress beginning January 3, 1949, and, during the next ten or twelve years, that trend more or less continued. Then—because of certain other developments, concluding with the war in Vietnam—the Congress objected and started to constrict the authority of the President, particularly in the area of foreign policy.

I vigorously oppose, as I did when I was President, certain restrictions enacted on appropriations bills and authorization bills tying the hands of a President—not only myself and my predecessor, but also, potentially, President Carter. The President, as commander in chief, is far more limited today than other Presidents in the history of the country in the day-to-day negotiations and the execution of foreign policy. And I think it is wrong. Something ought to be done about it.

IRVING KRISTOL, resident scholar, American Enterprise Institute: Mr. President, one of the phenomena we have witnessed in the past ten years is what some people call the "democratization of Congress," namely, the fact that the congressional leadership is not nearly so powerful today as it was, say, in Lyndon Johnson's day or even in your own. How does that affect a President's relations with Congress or how will it affect it?

PRESIDENT FORD: When I came to the Congress, Irving, Sam Rayburn and Joe Martin were alternating as speaker of the House, and, of course, Lyndon Johnson, with a party continuously in the majority, became the leader of the U.S. Senate.

When I served in the House, members would sometimes object to the way Sam Rayburn or Joe Martin spoke for the majority or the minority party, or, as speaker for the entire House. A member might think *he* had been elected just as the speaker had been and that the speaker should not have such prerogatives. But it was an orderly House, and the President could deal with that kind of arrangement and that kind of leadership in an effective way.

7

Then, the pendulum swung, and the House became more "democratized." The members felt that they had gained more active participation, but the President found it much more difficult to deal with 535 people, rather than with the speaker and the leaders of the two political parties. Relations between the Congress and the executive branch became strained, in many cases, I think, unnecessarily, and the job was getting done less effectively because no President can deal with 535 members, or even with half that number.

I oftentimes wished, when I was President, that the leaders could carry out what I knew was their view. But, when I was President, the members of the House had become more independent, and the leaders no longer had the power that Sam Rayburn had.

To summarize, when I was President, I would have liked Congress to be the way Sam Rayburn, or Lyndon Johnson, or Joe Martin ran it. When I was a House member—one of the troops, not a leader—I would have preferred it the way it is today.

ROBERT BORK, resident scholar, American Enterprise Institute: Mr. President, we have mentioned what might be viewed as the incursion of the Congress into the President's responsibilities in foreign affairs. Are there signs that the same thing is happening in the domestic area—in the enormous bureaucracy on the hill, which oversees so much of the executive branch, and in the General Accounting Office, which is taking over what looks like executive functions in the creation of independent agencies?

PRESIDENT FORD: When I was in the House, Bob, I used to say the House committees needed more staff, that staffs would be invaluable in advising House members and committee chairmen or ranking minority members. I think there was a need back in the 1950s, because our staffs were relatively small, although very expert.

Citizens complain about the growth of the federal government, but they should differentiate between the branches. The number of civilians in the executive branch of the government has been more or less level. But the growth in the number of staff people in the Congress has been about ten times the growth of GNP, that is, of any other aspect of our society.

I must say, I think it has gotten out of hand. To a substantial degree, these staff people are now having more impact on the Congress, both the Senate and the House, than their position justifies. Somebody has to take a look at that situation—it has gotten out of hand.

ROBERT KLITZMAN, student: Mr. President, you came to the office of President through the office of vice president. I am curious about what your impressions were of this office, what you feel the function and role of the vice presidency is with relation to the President, and whether or not you think it should be changed.

PRESIDENT FORD: I was vice president in a unique period, so I would rather comment on the basis of the vice president I had in Nelson Rockefeller.

First, I selected him because I thought he would be an outstanding President if he ever became President. Second, I had a good working relationship with him because he was an active man, he was an experienced person, and he had good judgment.

I gave him many, many specific assignments. For example, when we were called upon to look at some of the abuses in the intelligence community—and I use that term in the broadest sense—the Congress was investigating it, in both the House and the Senate. I felt that we ought to have a high-level commission look at the CIA and the related intelligence agencies, so I appointed Vice President Rockefeller to head a seven-man commission made up of outstanding people. He was also given a responsibility to look into the personnel problems, the pay, and so forth, in the executive branch of the government, and an excellent report resulted.

I think a vice president can be used to add prestige to an investigation or the handling of a problem, so that everybody knows it is a matter of deep concern to the President. A vice president has the constitutional responsibility of presiding over the Senate, of course, but he can be used in many, many other ways, as Nelson Rockefeller was. I think he did a superior job in every assignment he was given.

I do not think it is possible to lay out a schedule of what the vice president is going to do for four years. The President simply has to assure him, and he has to be willing to cooperate on any tough job that the President wants him to do. That's what we did.

CHRIS HOWE, student: Mr. President, do you think it is wise for the President to speak openly about matters of foreign policy and negotiation, or do you think that such discussion would impede negotiations between bargaining powers?

PRESIDENT FORD: I think only time will tell which technique, or which procedure, or which tactic or strategy is the right one. When I was President, we used one such approach, and President Carter is using another. It is too early to judge, and I do not think at this time

I should comment on the new technique or strategy. Events will determine which was the better way.

DAVID GRACE, student: Many special interest groups carry on quite an active lobbying campaign here in Washington. Is there a way the President can guarantee that a more general or national viewpoint will enter into executive decision making, or will it always have not quite enough influence in decision making?

PRESIDENT FORD: The Constitution provides that people have the right to petition. That does not mean individuals only; it also means the organizations they belong to. I don't think we will ever get away from that right, and I don't think it could be denied them, individually or collectively.

Some organizations are more effective than others, and the ones you are speaking of are probably the most effective ones, whether you agree with them or not. As a congressman, I always used to open the door and let them come in and state their case. Sometimes they would give me a refreshing viewpoint, contrary to the bureaucracy within the government, and I think that is healthy. Or they would have different viewpoints from other lobbying organizations on the same subject.

As long as they are kept at arm's length and just allowed to talk or to make their point, I don't see anything wrong with them. But if members of Congress become more involved, they can get into some difficulty.

MR. KRISTOL: Mr. President, one of the problems that students of American government are perplexed about at the moment is who, if anyone, will control the federal bureaucracy. Congress seems unable to control all of it. Originally, the President was thought to be the person to control it, but that seems to have changed. Is it possible to control this bureaucracy at all, or will it end up being an independent branch of government?

PRESIDENT FORD: Let me make one categorical statement. We have about 2,100,000 federal civilian employees, and I would say some 90 percent of them are able, dedicated, highly qualified people. What I say about the system does not apply to the individuals in it.

Congress certainly does not control them. In fact, I think one can honestly say that over the last five years, Congress has created more bureaucracy by enacting legislation that mandates certain expenditures for more personnel. The Congress has made no honest effort to reduce the bureaucracy. In effect, by the laws it passed and the appropriations it imposed on Presidents, Congress increased the problem. The blame for the bureaucracy, I think, falls on the Congress. And the laws that have been passed make it very, very difficult—as I'm sure Bob Bork knows—to get rid of even the incompetent members of the executive branch. They are protected almost unbelievably.

In my judgment, the Congress is primarily responsible, not only for the number of people employed, but also for the rules and regulations under which a President or the cabinet officers are not allowed to replace people. If my recollection is accurate, out of 2,100,000 people that work in the civilian side of the federal government, a new President can appoint only about 2,000, which is a very low proportion. I think a President ought to have a little more flexibility further down in the bureaucracy, as to both the people appointed and those that can be dismissed.

The American voters select a President because of what he says or promises, or his philosophy, but, if he cannot reach into the bowels of a department, his decisions way up at the top will seldom be adequately implemented out in the grass roots. A President ought to have more flexibility, but Congress, I think, is going the other way.

DR. RANNEY: Mr. President, I wonder if it might not be interesting for a minute to lift our focus from this town and from the two ends of Pennsylvania Avenue. I would like to ask you this: As you look back, when did you feel the greatest frustration in trying to explain your analysis of a major public problem to the American people, and in trying to get them to accept your remedy for that problem?

PRESIDENT FORD: The most frustrating problem—the one I felt saddest about not solving quickly—was the unemployment problem. It resulted from the recession that began almost immediately after I became President.

Unemployment went from about 5½ percent when I became President to about 8 percent, the highest figure during the forty years since World War II. Some of the things that might have been done to try to win the battle against those statistics would have been very bad in the long run. A President cannot just turn a switch in the society in which we live and end unemployment—at least, not on a constructive basis. I suppose Uncle Sam could go out and hire all of the unemployed, or most of them, but I think most people would agree that is not the answer.

That was my most frustrating experience. Every month, the statistics would come out. We got the unemployment figures down from

7.5 to 7.2, and that looked encouraging, but then they started to go the other way.

I grew up in the Depression, and I went to high school with many young people whose fathers were unemployed. In those days, unemployment rose to 14 and 15 percent, and there was no social security program. There was no welfare program, as we know it today. There was no food stamp program. And so, hardship was really hardship in those days. I would say 25 percent of the fathers and mothers of my high school classmates were unemployed. It was a tough time. I understood the problems from personal experience, and, yet, there was nothing that I could do instantaneously to change it. We had to work our way out, and I think we were well on our way at the time I left the White House.

DR. RANNEY: Just to follow up on that, did you have the feeling, sir, that you and your administration were being blamed for the statistics unfairly? As we all know, there is a considerable time lag after policies are adopted. They make no visible impact for a year or eighteen months. Or did you feel that it was only the statistics that were getting the public attention?

PRESIDENT FORD: I became President on August 9, 1974. I think the economic circumstances that existed then foredoomed the recession that developed in early 1975. And I believe that the economic policies we carried out, as difficult as they were to sell—though we were able to get them reasonably well in place—will be very helpful to the present President. He is now reaping the harvest of some good policies we carried out, just as I inherited some that led to inflation of 12 percent or more and an economic recession which was right on our doorstep. But that is what happens in this society, and thank goodness we do not try to solve all the problems by government action. We let our economic system solve them in the long run.

MR. BORK: I want to return to the subject that Mr. Kristol raised about the bureaucracy. I quite agree that the President needs more control over the bureaucracy, but is it true that, even with a change in the law, there are just too many regulations and too many decisions being made by regulators for a President to keep up with them effectively?

PRESIDENT FORD: No President could, under any circumstances, read all the regulations that come out. I do not see how a cabinet officer can, in all honesty, do that, isolated within his own department.

We made a major effort to deregulate some of the economic segments of our society—the airline industry, the trucking industry, and the railroad industry. Some regulatory bodies, after they have been in existence for a time, develop their own little constituency—not only the people they regulate but also the lawyers that come before them and live quite well on what they earn from their clients. In many respects, the regulatory agencies are a little incestuous with the people they regulate and the lawyers that benefit from their clients' problems.

In those three cases, we tried at least to break the trend and to start on a better way. I was glad to see that President Carter has embraced and endorsed what we proposed in the deregulation of the airline industry. I hope his administration is successful in getting through what we, unfortunately, were not able to, while I was President.

MR. SIEGEL: Mr. President, as you know both the presidency and the man, what do you feel were the root causes of President Nixon's downfall? Does a President need to be actively on the lookout to avoid those problems?

PRESIDENT FORD: I would rather not, if you will excuse me, get into any discussion of Mr. Nixon's problems. But let me just relate the question to my own experiences.

I think a President has to have absolute faith and trust in the individuals he picks to work in his administration. He should not have to look over their shoulders every day to see that they are doing the right job, if he has selected the right people. I think we had a good cabinet, one of the best since I have been in Washington, so I did not have to worry about abuses, or illegal actions, or things that were, perhaps, unethical. And I think that is what a President has to do. If he gets the right people to work for him, then, the dangers that arose in several administrations won't pop up.

MR. DEVANE: Mr. President, most recent Presidents can be defined in terms of the psychological impact they had on the nation—you, for returning morality to government and Presidents Johnson and Nixon for relatively demoralizing effects. Considering that this impact really cannot be perceived until a man gets into office, how can we define the capacity for, say, inspirational leadership in candidates for the presidency?

PRESIDENT FORD: That is a very tough question. I don't think we can draft a prescription that says this man, as a candidate, will be a good President. But, looking over the thirty-eight Presidents, I think the American people have, regardless of political affiliation, selected men who met the test. There are always exceptions, but it has been a pretty good system overall, in the last two hundred years. I repeatedly say I have a lot of faith in the good judgment of the American people. Once in a while they make a mistake, but overall their batting average is pretty good.

MR. KLITZMAN: Mr. President, do you think it is possible for one man to leave a permanent mark on the institution of the presidency, and, if so, how do you think you left a stamp on that office?

PRESIDENT FORD: The most difficult problem we inherited was the total division within the country, the angry mood, the turmoil, plus a number of very serious international problems. Over a period of time, by keeping cool and getting good people to do the job in each and every department, we dissipated the angry attitude that people had toward government and toward one another.

If I were to write my own summary, that would be what I am most proud of and what I would want history to record as an achievement of the administration.

MR. STONE: Mr. President, what would be the best governmental experience for someone entering the White House?

PRESIDENT FORD: I think it is highly important to get a broad education. I am going back to my alma mater, at Ann Arbor, for four days to meet with students and faculty. I was reminded the other day that when I was in college, as some of you are, I studied a number of courses in American government. The head of the Political Science Department there checked my grade, which I had forgotten, and I had done well.

I think a President has to have an education. He has to expect to serve long and hard without a great monetary reward. Nobody should expect to make a lot of money, legally at least, in public service, and I wouldn't want anything except honesty and integrity in your service. Then, a President has to have an interest in working on other people's problems.

If a person does not have an education, an interest in people, and a willingness to serve, he should not get into government, because that is what government is really all about. He can make a good living in government, but he is not going to be wealthy when he is through.

MR. SIEGEL: Every year, the federal government overspends—has a deficit. What would you think of taking private savings and excess corporate profits and using them to subsidize the federal deficit?

PRESIDENT FORD: In the first place, there are some problems of definition. What are *excess* profits? Ever since I came to Congress, I have heard people say we have to have an excess profits tax. Well, during the Korean War I think, Congress passed an excess profits tax, and it turned out to be a total flop. It's a long story why, but it comes down to a matter of definition.

In the minds of many people, our federal tax rates on corporate profits are too excessive for us to accumulate capital and expand our economy to provide jobs. I don't accept the premise that profits are excessive in this country, across the board. An industry or a particular company might do extremely well, but over the years those profits will average out.

In regard to private savings, who do you think buys securities today? They are bought from private savings, whether directly in federal bonds or through financial institutions that buy the bonds that make up the deficit. In effect, that is what happens today. Is my economic analysis correct? I think it is.

I would rather get to the fundamental problem, which is to achieve a balanced budget within a reasonable number of years. And it is possible, if we do not kowtow and accept every spending program that some special interest group wants to foist on the rest of the citizens of this country.

One of the most serious problems we have is the excessive rate of growth of the federal government. In January 1976, we made a study that showed the rate of growth of the federal expenditures for the previous decade was 11 percent. When we extrapolated that for the next twenty-five years, we found that the taxes paid by people and the borrowings by the federal government inevitably would change our total system of government. We tried to cut the rate of growth of federal government expenditures from 11 percent per annum to about 5½ percent, which is a sustainable, reasonable rate of growth. That rate would have led to a balanced budget, we said, by 1979, and that would have given us a reasonable cushion and some security and control over the next few years.

MR. KRISTOL: Mr. President, what do you think of the future of the cabinet as a collective institution? Does it make any sense to get these department heads—experts from very different fields, with very different interests—sitting around together and talking?

PRESIDENT FORD: I think it is important to have those departments, or some variations of them, and they should be headed by top people. On the other hand, we run into problems that do not fit into this department or that department. Take energy, for example. The Department of Interior and the Department of Treasury become involved in energy decisions, for one reason or another, as well as independent agencies such as the Energy Research and Development Agency and the Federal Energy Administration.

When we had an issue that fell into three or four departments or independent agencies, we formed "a cabinet level ad hoc committee." For example, we had an energy committee composed of three or four cabinet officers and several others. The head of the Department of Interior, Rogers Morton, was the head of the Cabinet Task Force. That was how we handled one problem.

We could solve a problem that way in the executive branch because the President could tell five people to get together with one of them as chairman. But let me tell you about a more serious problem. Take the energy situation. I sent up to the Capitol a thick energy program involving thirteen basic proposals, for oil and natural gas, nuclear energy, coal, et cetera. We put it all in one bill because my experience on the Hill led me to believe that was the best way to do it.

The Congress should have analyzed that problem in one committee. Instead, what did they do? They took the portion that involved nuclear power and tore off those pages and sent them to the Joint Atomic Energy Committee. They tore off the next section, which involved, say coal, and that went to another committee. And they tore off the part that involved offshore development, and that went to another committee. About ten different committees ended up trying to solve a problem that should have been analyzed by a single committee.

Unfortunately, that system in the House and the Senate has contributed significantly to the lack of action in solving the energy problem. I hope that, when Mr. Carter's program goes up to the Hill, the House and Senate will each have a single committee drawn from all those other committees—just one committee to do the investigating, call the witnesses, make the recommendations.

MS. BARON: Mr. President, what are your views on the electoral college as a viable institution for selecting the President?

PRESIDENT FORD: In 1969 or 1970, I voted to recommend to the states a constitutional amendment that would call for the election of a

President by a majority of the popular vote in the country. The bill would have done away with the electoral college. I supported it and spoke for it on the floor of the House, and it passed by better than a two-to-one margin, which is necessary, of course. The bill went over to the Senate, and it got tied up in a filibuster there.

I am on record, and my basic views have not changed. I came to that conclusion about the electoral college after studying what had happened on the two or three occasions when there was not a majority in the electoral college for one candidate.

I was talking to Austin Ranney earlier about the election in 1804 and the ones in 1824 and in 1876. There was one case when the politicians in the House of Representatives rather than the people selected the President. If we get into that problem again, the people rather than the politicians ought to make the selection.

MR. BORK: Mr. President, earlier you said that you thought the President was being increasingly constrained by Congress in the field of foreign affairs, which, I take it, would make the President less capable of reacting quickly. Have you seen any evidence that our allies are discouraged by their recognition of the diminution of presidential power, or that our adversaries are encouraged and more adventuresome?

PRESIDENT FORD: I think that both conclusions are inevitable—both by our friends and by our adversaries—because they are legitimate conclusions. If a President of the United States, the most powerful nation in the world, cannot act with speed and determination in a military crisis, that would inevitably encourage the adversary and raise concern among our allies. Congress ought to get off the President's back in the field of foreign policy. Congress can declare war; the President cannot declare war. The President is commander in chief according to the Constitution. Congress cannot be commander in chief. The Congress ought to exercise its own responsibilities and let the President do his job under the Constitution. I do not agree with those in Congress who said during the war in Vietnam that Congress had not approved it or had no opportunity to disapprove. It did. Every year, in the authorization bill and the appropriation bill for the Department of Defense, it could have voted against the war. From 1959 or thereabouts—and accelerating from 1961 and 1962—Congress could have done any of a number of things, if it had wanted to terminate our involvement. During that whole span of time, it did nothing adverse to the Presidents who handled our problems. In fact, there was some affirmative action by Congress, the Gulf of Tonkin Resolution being one example.

I think Congress just got carried away, and I hope it returns to a policy that is more in the best interest of the country.

PROFESSOR GREENSTEIN: One institution we have not discussed yet, which obviously bears on everything you have been discussing, is the press and the mass media. Could you remark briefly on your views, both on whether you felt you got a fair shake in day-by-day coverage and on whether you considered the format of the debates adequate for communicating to the American people?

PRESIDENT FORD: I always had good personal relations with members of the press when I was in Congress and when I was vice president and President. That does not mean that they agreed with me or that I agreed with them. That does not mean I liked every story I saw or every headline I read. I am sure they did not like some of the decisions I made, but we had a good personal relationship in ninety-nine cases out of a hundred. I understood their responsibilities, and they understood mine.

On the average, I received as good treatment as any President could expect. No President should expect to like every morning newspaper he reads over his span of service, whether it is four years or less. In fact, one of the luxuries of being out of office is to read the morning newspaper and say, "Gee, I'm glad I have no involvement with that mess in Washington." That is usually the way the press writes it, because a headline that is dismal or dramatic is better than one about the good things that take place. Even though we liked one another—and I think we did, in the main—I did not expect the press to write nice things just because we had a good personal relationship.

You asked about the debates. I think they ought to be institutionalized in the campaign. As to whether the format we used in 1976 is the best, I have not studied it in detail or looked at other options. I have no real objection to the way the debates were done, and I have heard of no alternative that would convince me to change the format.

MR. KLITZMAN: Mr. President, how often do you rely on your own conscience in making decisions, and how often do you rely on various pressure groups, whether they be Congress, or the courts, or the press and mass media, or lobbying groups? What do you feel should be the relationship between these different pressure groups and your own conscience?

PRESIDENT FORD: It is hard to be totally certain whether conscience or some other factor matters most. Some subjective feelings about certain things or certain issues are bound to play a part. In my case, I had a combination of what I thought were good recommendations from people in the administration and my own background and personal convictions. It was a combination of the two—options that came to me and my own experience and convictions—that ended up in whatever decision I made.

PROFESSOR GREENSTEIN: Thank you, Mr. President.

PRESIDENT FORD: Thank you. It was nice to be here, and I appreciate the chance to answer some questions.

LIST OF PARTICIPANTS

Gerald R. Ford, the thirty-eighth President of the United States, and the Distinguished Fellow of the American Enterprise Institute

Robert Bork, AEI resident scholar and former solicitor general of the United States

Irving Kristol, AEI resident scholar and coeditor of *The Public Interest*

Austin Ranney, AEI resident scholar and former president of the American Political Science Association

Fred I. Greenstein, Henry Luce professor of law, politics, and society, Princeton University

And students of Professor Greenstein's course on the American presidency:

> *Jill Baron*
>
> *Bob Chartener*
>
> *Richard Devane*
>
> *David Grace*
>
> *Chris Howe*
>
> *Robert Klitzman*
>
> *Jeff Siegel*
>
> *Warren Stone*

Cover and book design: Pat Taylor

SELECTED 1977 PUBLICATIONS TO DATE

A Discussion with Gerald R. Ford: The American Presidency records the reflections of the thirty-eighth President of the United States on the formidable responsibilities of the chief executive. On the occasion of his first return to Washington after leaving the presidency, Gerald R. Ford meets with a group of scholars and students in a candid exchange on the powers and limitations of the office. Among the questions raised in this discussion are: Is the bureaucracy in Congress taking over executive functions? Can a woman become President? Should the electoral college be abolished? Do the media treat the President fairly? And how can a President leave a stamp on the office?

In his answers to these questions, the former President makes the following remarks:

"A President has to have an interest in working on other people's problems. If a person does not have an education, an interest in people, and a willingness to serve, he should not get into government, because that is what government is really all about."

"The pressures were not nearly as severe as I expected."

"The President, as commander in chief, is far more limited today than other Presidents in the history of the country. . . . And I think that is wrong."

"The laws that have been passed make it very, very difficult to get rid of even the incompetent members of the executive branch. They are protected almost unbelievably."

Joining in the discussion are Robert Bork, Irving Kristol, and Austin Ranney, all resident scholars of the American Enterprise Institute, and Professor Fred I. Greenstein, Henry Luce professor of politics, law, and society at Princeton University, together with students from his course on the presidency.

$1.25

 American Enterprise Institute for Public Policy Research
1150 Seventeenth Street, N.W., Washington, D.C. 20036